UNPRACTICAL THINKING

Arne Weingart

Thanks to the following publications where poems have previously appeared:

"A Death on Facebook," *Mayday Magazine*
"Amazonomachy," *ARTlines Anthology*, Museum of Fine Arts, Houston
"Erasure," *Solstice Literary Magazine*
"Leaf," *Mudfish*
Norman Frank," *Oberon*
"Piecework," *The Southeast Review*
"Smoke, Hats," "Dolmens, Menhirs, Cromlechs," *Southern Poetry Review*
"The Old Poets in Line at the Urinals at the Writers' Conference," *Paterson Literary Review*
"The Poet Decides to Stop Writing," "The Painting of the Barn without the Barn," *Nimrod Journal*
"The Weather on Mars," *Passager*
"Trainwreck, Minneapolis (A Love Poem)," *New Millennium Writings*

ISBN 978-1-7326501-7-6
Printed in the United States of America

RED MOUNTAIN PRESS

Santa Fe, New Mexico
www.redmountainpress.us

"S'il vous plaît...dessine-moi un mouton!"

– "Le Petit Prince," Antoine de Saint-Exupéry

Also by Arne Weingart:

Levitation for Agnostics

III

I

SMOKE, HATS

My father wore a hat and smoked if he was awake.
He wore a hat mowing the lawn in his undershirt
and smoked lying down and standing up. He smoked

at the table. He smoked like he meant it. He did
mean it. Smoking didn't kill him any more than
wearing a hat killed him. Something else killed him.

Something else. I don't know what killed him.
Do you remember what killed him? Something else.
I won't wear a hat outside. I don't wear a hat unless

my ears are falling off in the cold and my breath is
like smoke. Just like smoke. I don't wear a yarmulke
in temple because I want God to see me, the one

who's not wearing a yarmulke, if God should need
to see me. But I don't go to temple often. I hardly ever
go to temple. If God wants to find me he could look

for my breath like white smoke in the cold. Or he
could look for the one whose ears are about to fall off,
the one walking fast, wishing he had remembered his hat.

ERASURE

The branch, when I
    pry it up out of the ice

on the patio because
    I mean to let it dry and

set it on fire for its
    negligible quantum of heat,

leaves a foliate negative
    that melts and fades,

the only image of itself
    it will have ever surrendered,

like leaf prints
    on a sidewalk or

indecipherable graffiti on
    the previously never-noticed walls.

Absence, being infinite, is
    what sticks, what enthralls.

The sun itself
    will have to count on

the memory of
    surviving stars when

approximately eight billion years
    from approximately now

it has its last day
    and falls into the always

night, those sister stars
    who knew their little brother

when he was obnoxiously
    hot, unmercifully bright.

Memory is what we have
    until memory fades away.

SNAGGING SALMON

It starts with the alewives in the Great Lakes,
having snuck in, just like my emigrant relatives,
from the Atlantic via the Hudson, succeeding beyond the

wildest collective dream herrings can have until they suddenly
begin to die off in the millions, washing up on all the August
    beaches
of Chicago in stinking windrows, clogging the water intake

tunnels, making it impossible to ride down Lakeshore Drive
with the windows open. The answer, obvious to all,
is to stock the Lakes with Chinook salmon from Oregon,

anadromous alewife eaters who will get fat and happy
living in the Midwest, who will invest their own precious lives
in the sport fishing business, so glad you asked them.

The salmon hatchlings are dumped in their silvery
millions from huge white PVC buckets into the inlets,
lagoons and harbors that ring Lake Michigan,

each point of departure having its own special smell,
the one thing that draws the salmon back when, like
teenagers in heat, they discover the need to spawn

and thus come swimming in their multitudes
back into the Lincoln Park Lagoon, the place they
best remember the smell of, where they are snagged

by a heavy duty treble hook in the flank or tail or gills
and yanked out of the water to thrash and die in a huge
white PVC bucket by men who come at daybreak

to stand in the November cold on the banks of the Lagoon
and troll furiously for the red fish flesh of the Pacific Northwest,
their lines continually fouled by the Canada Geese practicing

migratory take-offs and landings and by permanent resident
ducks and by apologetic late season scullers getting their last
sessions in on the water. The fish go home not as trophies

but to be eaten, even though they themselves contain
parts per million of white PVC microplastic particles
which will end up as parts per million in some of us,

will go with us to our graves, not as proximate cause,
not that we can tell, but as effect, as reminder of what we can
never fully hope to know, as avatar and artifact of smell.

POET DESCENDING A STAIRCASE

The logical thing would be couplets, one
line for each foot and so on until you get to

the landing where your love is waiting,
naked as you are, except it turns out
there are an odd number of steps so you

climb back to the top, so sorry, and try to
figure out whether tercets will get you
where you need to go or some odd
combination of couplets, tercets, quatrains,

anything that gives the appearance of
intentional art, but not having counted
stairs on the way back up you have no
freaking idea how to get to the bottom
of things without falling insouciantly down

the entire flight, your head clipping the
banister balusters like a xylophone and your
arms and legs changing places continuously
as if in a cubist cartoon which they in fact
are in while you try to keep smiling that same
smile which your love once said in different

circumstances, never to be repeated after
tonight, she found impossible to resist.

LIGHT PROP FOR AN ELECTRIC STAGE

for László Moholy-Nagy

Everything can be photographed.
Every photograph can be explained.
Every explanation can be painted on white gesso with
      permanent paint.
Every painting can be thought of, at least for argument's sake,
      as flat sculpture.
And every sculpture can be placed on a stage, waiting for its
      music, its light,
its scenery, its incurably conflicted actors who will tell its sad,
      wonderful story.

I had a story once, it was a lie about the past, but filled with
      convincing detail –
the bongos, the guitars, the disheveled bedroom,
      the forced march
to a distant village – but lies about the past
are only useful as practice for lying about the future,
which is the necessary and inescapable condition
      of consciousness,
something dogs and parakeets don't have to bother with.

We, on the other hand,
love to see our lies about the future
fight each other to the death under the proscenium arch
or else embrace with obscene propinquity at the end of the
      second act,
all the while bathed in bright geometric light,
which is how we imagine the future signs its name
on all our uncommitted acts.

WILD MAN

New video footage from a drone shows the first images of members of an isolated Amazon tribe that had no known contact with the outside world, the Brazilian government said this week.
– The New York Times, August 23, 2018

We see him from above at some distance

moving through a clearing carrying
what appears to be a spear, we're not sure.
Although the drone cannot have been

completely silent he does not look up

but moves normally as if this, too, were normal.
The drone is not allowed to fly lower
or worse, to follow, which would break the rule

we all now understand, which is that we

are contagious, that we are a disease
he and all his tribe will never recover from.
First will come canned goods, then medicine,

a motor for the back of his canoe,

then dresses, shoes and trousers, alcohol,
and the worst pathogen, a new alphabet
whereby his language will be parsed into
mere linguistics. Walking there below,

carrying what appears to be a spear,
his life completely strung on sight and sound
as though on wire that reaches back centuries,

I don't believe he hasn't seen or heard us.
I think he has a word for what we are,
another word for what he now must do.

Seasonal, an Ode

Deadheading the geraniums,
what am I prepared to miss most?
That scent of green on my fingers
and, now the summer is done for,
their perfervid insistence on red,
red, yet more red before
I decide to stop watering them.

I am not in love with the natural world.
It's the unnatural world I worry about,
the late bloomers, the unnaturally early
risers, all the instances of life imitating art
imitating life. I love what lingers
unreasonably long past its season.

Who among us is not cultivar?
And what was the purpose, exactly,
of the hyper-extended tailfins
on the '57 Impala, other than to
fill me with disappointment and desire?

So what if we end up unlovely embers
in a fire we didn't set? It's time
to stop whining and prepare
for the worst, to turn on the lights
the way we always turn on the lights
to welcome the unreluctant approach
of nightfall.

       If you listen hard,
no matter how bad your ears are,
you can hear the sky and all its air
turn cold and occasionally concussive.
Are you ready for some football?

DOLMENS, MENHIRS, CROMLECHS

We need one of these, I think to
myself, something solid, indivisible,
to demonstrate how we sought to
align ourselves with the tide of

history, the phases of the moon
landing, the low-orbiting satellites
from which we receive our sense
of self. Although our quantum

understanding of matter has us
convinced that even the densest,
most indifferent stone is mostly
anti-matter, we need something

standing in an open field, while
there are still open fields, to remind
us of who we were. We will have
gotten it wrong, no doubt, we will

have failed to protect our crops,
consecrate our water, keep our
children from making our same
mistakes. Let others judge. Let

them try, centuries hence, to
divine our fatal misunderstandings.
Let others shake their heads
in wonder. Let there be others.

The Painting of the Barn Without the Barn

for Joan Snyder

In order to paint the painting of the barn
without the barn you must first give up

the rectangle, which would have been
useful as a tool for scale, proportion,

position on the canvas, general uprightness,
flatness, thingness, off which the light

of a normal day might be reflected. You must
also bid regretful farewell to the bean fields

surrounding the barn. Even the rolling hills
of your neighbor's property in the far

northeast corner of your frame and their
possible contribution to perspective must be

gainsaid in favor of the idea of the barn,
the idea of the color of the barn and what

shape that idea takes if it is meant to contain
the idea of small, useful animals, the idea of hay.

Eventually you begin to paint. Eventually
the ideas find their favorite colors and arrange

themselves the way notes arrange themselves
on the page for someone who has never read music.

ELECTIVE AFFINITIES

Goldfinch to sunflower
badger to grass
what is it binds
like to like
so that the planet
all planets
are permitted to
go on spinning
what is it drives
the orange housecat
down to the riverbank
at midday to stalk
what lies hidden
in fern and vine
what ancient hunt
lies sealed in
her ancient heart
what is it binds
you to me
so that mouth
to mouth arm
on arm we walk
through every door
that still opens

TERMS OF SURRENDER

I wish to negotiate.
While I still have a horse saddled and a man standing.
While I have arrows and, yes, archers.
While my planes are up in the air and circling, circling.
While my finger hovers over the button.

I can accept defeat.
I've had practice, haven't we all?
I can be gracious, self-deprecating,
fully appreciative of consequence,
of the general necessity of this turn of events.

I'm a realist.
We're all realists here.
Reality is our new religion. We can't get enough reality.
But even if the battle is still in question, the war is over.
I know it. You know it. The grass with its new coat
of human ash and the river now gap-toothed with its missing
    bridges know it.

So, what I would like is to walk away gracefully,
whatever grace remains between us. I would like to participate in
dignified relinquishment even if it means the ritual humiliation
    of your choosing.
I would like to gather in a picturesque setting to discuss
    reparations and borders
and then retreat to a forgotten corner of my country,
there to write, to lie, to drink a little, to die. I would like
lots of history to be written, even if inaccurate. And I would like
an inscription in something obdurate, granite,
bronze, stainless. Perhaps a statue.

BORDERLINE

He moves in darkness as it seems to me,
Not of woods only and the shade of trees.
– Robert Frost, "The Mending Wall"

To not acknowledge the border
is a variety of disorder,
we are told, and I believe it,

although if it is real, as real as
blood and dirt, why would it require
believing? There is you and there is

me and there are all the others
who are not, those who perform
brain surgery, those with the

inexplicable tattoos, those who
stand around oil drums at night
in the underpasses on the outskirts

of medium-sized cities who have
nothing left to lose, those whose feet
fit comfortably in cowboy boots,

in ballerina shoes. They are all
across it, in a different state,
one I may never get around to

visiting even though they say
the weather is incomparable
in certain seasons. I would go there

in a minute just to get away
from where I am if not for the
credentials and the declarations

and the tricky questions concerning
your reasons for being there, not to
mention the lines which can be

unpredictable and long. For the
moment, I stay on this side,
meandering the wide aisles of

going-out-of-business bookstores,
seeing how the books no longer give
their shelves a reason for being.

COUNTERFACTUAL REGRET MINIMIZATION

We give the AI a description of the game. We don't tell it how to play," says Noam Brown, a [Carnegie Mellon University] grad student who built the system alongside his professor, Tuomas Sandholm. "It develops a strategy completely independently from human play, and it can be very different from the way humans play the game.
— "*Wired Magazine*," 2/1/17

In Heads-up No Limit Texas Hold'em
the number of information sets, or paths
of play, is ten to the power of one hundred
sixty or an order of magnitude greater
than the number of atoms in the universe.

Give or take. Add a few more players
around the table and complexity approaches
the infinite, something you or I, in all
probability, will never do, no matter how
complicated we think we are. Regret,

from this standpoint, would seem to be
an inevitable part of the game. There will
always have been a better move. Success
can only have been temporary. Your opponent,
despite his reputation and his winnings and

his seven-hundred-dollar sunglasses, can
never have been the best possible player.
One cannot help wishing the ability to
review one's options infinitely. One is
human. And even though one lies with

natural grace and bluffs like a reptile,
one will never achieve infinite regressivity,
that talent for minimization with regard to
one's own naked need possessed by certain
counting machines referred to as super.

The Suicide Returns to Leave a Note

This is for your benefit, not mine.
Although I can see how you might think
I felt I left something unsaid at the end.
But no. I said what I could say while I
was still alive. There are some who wonder,
maybe you're one, whether I have regrets,
whether, in those first few feet of fall,
I had second thoughts. I prefer
to no longer speak in metaphors.

Nothing is like anything else anymore.
There was a railing, an edge, a leap, a drop,
water hard as concrete, final consequences.
Life, I came to understand, is binary,
not some accumulation of missed opportunities
and best intentions, but a switch marked On
or Off. I chose Off, never having fully
understood the On position. Now
I know everything and nothing, which is
what all the great mystics used to brag about.
I guess some still do, to ever smaller audiences.
Still, I don't blame you for wanting to know
what might lie beyond or even in plain sight.

The answer, if I could give you one, which
I can't, might not even apply because
your afterward might be different from mine,
not having exited by the same door.
All I can tell you, which is still not much,
is that we try to let bygones be bygones.

Think of it like a club where it's considered
poor form to bring up bad luck or old money –
another metaphor – you'll have to pardon me
the way I pardoned you, not that you were
ever guilty of anything other than
wanting to go on living.

DREAMING IN YIDDISH

There are no native speakers
there are no natives
that land where
one could be born
in Yiddish
is no more
although dying
in dialect
is still possible

This is what happens
when your parents
set aside a whole language
for keeping secrets

We few who still
recognize the sound
of the vernacular
we never knew
speak to each other
exclusively in dreams
passing back and forth
memories of mud
and pasture
the smell of wet fur
letters from
cousins we'd never
recognize on the street

Asleep we are of one mind
in blaming our parents
for being so foreign
so unathletic

for running their whole
lives away from
the one and only
tongue that when they
needed their privacy
when they needed
relief from their own
broken English
they fell into backwards
like a pile of Bessarabian
oak leaves like a quilt
stuffed with the feathers
of countless Polish geese

FLOATING DOCK

In winter or   just before official calendrical winter
before the   lagoon chokes up on its own ice
    the   floating dock is detached from its bank
next to the   boathouse and set literally adrift
    there is no   place for it to go other than
the far bank of the   lagoon or a few feet north
    or south in its shallow   man-made ditch
just once I'd like to see it inch   out into the harbor
    so slow we'd never notice   and make its way
out into the lake then pick up   speed because
    who's to say it wouldn't   happen this way

navigate all the great   lakes and locks and
    sail like a   nondescript sloop down the
inland waterway   travel by night so as
    not to arouse the   suspicions of the fishermen
who flycast for dinner out   on the ends of their jetties
    then pull into some small   mosquito-cursed cove
on the Indian River to wait   out the season
    plenty of time left to   float in deep green water
where it never freezes   and where rowers
    morning and evening   never push off
never row home

The Lineup

Toward morning
while the night
argues with itself
about whether to let
the light in
a single dove
announces the day's schedule
birds
squirrels
more birds
lizards on their branches
in the full light of day
turtles
last birds
an armadillo
always late
for an appointment
and one small frog
sitting in the middle of the sidewalk
past midnight singing
to his own kind

II

THE POET DECIDES TO STOP WRITING

for Mark Strand

We could have guessed where you were headed,
I suppose, even from your early work, with its

Focus on the edge of the page, the comforting
Distance between people and other people, things

And other things. But even liminality, an entire
Lifetime of it, has limits. It would take someone

As determined and crafty as you to figure out
How to start unsaying, in that consistent, understated

Style, what you've already said. Perhaps you
Started not writing too late to undo what you wanted

Undone. Or was it mainly your intention to
Slowly start the planet rotating in the opposite direction

On its same and only axis? We are taught early on,
If we happened to have been paying attention,

That in the world of real numbers, every integer
Has its real and necessary negative. There are

Alternative universes, populated only by
Mathematical necessity, made plausible by what

We have discovered we may not know. This is
Where all the unwritten poems go, traveling out

From here, one by one, converging with what you
Always suspected, although unseen, we just might need.

THE ANNUAL WORKMEN'S CIRCLE PICNIC, SUMMER, 1955, IN A FIELD OUTSIDE NASHVILLE

Exactly how they picked the field I'll never know,

far enough away from anything
you could call a road so that several

minutes of involuntary bouncing

were required, nearly my favorite part
of the whole day, next to the hot dogs,

which had more bite in them the way Yiddish

contains more vowels and consonants, and my first
taste of beer, which, although Schlitz and foul,

was undeniably cold and important.

How my sister made it through the day
I'll never know, what with no friends and nothing

to do but pitch horseshoes and play poker

and throw a ball at wooden bottles
for a kewpie doll or a stuffed panda,

both of which she was far too old for,

and try to stay out of the sun and put off going
to the portable to pee, which would be

impossible since everyone was looking.

Everyone looked old to me and used up
in this field out in the country, but happy,

just how happy I'll never know, happy

not to be dead in Poland or Ukraine, happy
to have found a place to have children in,

strange and plausible,

a place to pitch a tent at the end of summer.
This is how I came to be here

or anywhere, a group of men deciding

that Nashville needed one more Jewish tailor
to come stand in this field with his family,

to drink his beer, to be nothing exceptional.

THE WEATHER ON MARS

for Zoe and Isaac

You'll say that everything is more or less
the same, the way you usually do,
although we can't help hearing the reports
that filter back to us, belatedly,

of conflagrations of dust and vapor ice
in the Noachis Quadrant, your last known
destination. We'd guess by now you have
undoubtedly moved on to Syrtis Major

or perhaps even as far as Elysium,
which sounds pleasant enough from this great distance.
We have no sense of scale or of the range
of reds our common sun surrenders in

your dawns, any of which would help us feel
closer, although not close, not now, not yet.
We shouldn't blame you for our failed attempts
to understand sea level where there is

no sea, where all the local hills shoulder
Everest aside, where love is absolute
and chance has consequences we could never
accommodate, however much we've seen

ourselves and been or hoped to be. We think
we know what can be known about the way
life turns toward life. But you are in a place
we never would have thought it possible

to be accustomed to. Some night, out on
Bradbury Landing or Glenelg, look down,
through all the planetary cold, at us
as we look up, as we look up at you

DOORBELL

The new doorbell has eyes and ears,
thin skin, the ability to detect motion,
intent, what is truly in the heart of
those who come to stand at my door,
is connected to all its sister and brother
doorbells who whisper continually
among themselves about intruders,
strangers, thieves, and dog-walkers who
let loose their hounds in the postage
stamp front garden to do as they will,
but strangely, predictably perhaps,
does not quite fit on the door. Take

this doorbell and put it in your purse,
which has room for at least a dozen
more doorbells, and carry it with you,
love. Take it out sometime in the middle
of the day, if you happen to think,
and push the button. Oh it's you,
I will say, how nice of you to come
calling. Wherever you are, love,
open the door and come in.

Norman Frank

On the way to work late
                 we drive past the Aston Martin showroom
on Clark Street where there is only ever
                       a single saleswoman,
hair done up tight with
               two fetching tendrils against her temples,
as if to signal room for negotiation
                    on options of which there are many,
snug pastel suit, four-inch heels.
                You have seen her in your dreams
a hundred times saying no.
             Of all the people who could actually buy this car,
who could begin to appreciate it
               the way it needs to be appreciated,
know it the way it needs to be known
                better than Norman Frank,
lonely 12-year-old explaining to me,
               lonely 11-year-old, what is important
in life? The Aston Martin is important,
               its engine displacement, its drive train,
its steering linkage, its exotic exhaust configuration,
                   even its obscene
leather interior said to be better than sex,
               whatever sex may end up being.
But perhaps not as important as the Bugatti,
              or Ferrari, or Lamborghini,
any of which, when you dare to say them,
             makes you instantly older.
And none more important than the Facel Vega,
              French cult car owned by
Ava Gardner, Dean Martin, Stirling Moss,
             the Shah of Iran, Ringo Starr,
the King of Morocco, François Truffaut,
            and the Marchioness of Tavistock,
among others. Also, important,
           American cars, all of them, and airplanes,
any. Norman Frank's father had a way
            of pronouncing gefilte fish
with four extra syllables that made it
           unrepeatable as well as inedible,

which we already knew. Gefilte fish was from
                              the old country, along with
Norman Frank's mother
                 whose name was Ilse and who never looked
anything other than sad but
                       who knew a little Polish and could therefore
sharpen up my mother's accent
                      from time to time. Norman Frank's father
died suddenly, heart attack I heard
                       but did not understand, maybe it was
the extra syllables that made his heart explode,
                              and they moved away
before I got a chance to ask about
                 Norman's cousin Anne, of whose existence
and non-existence I was not yet aware.
                       Can you imagine Anne Frank
in America, deciding what is important
                       and not important, beginning to
form the conviction that
                 in the names of things we invent the next century?

This is the poem,
no, wait a minute, this is the poem
with the false starts, the one that,
as soon as you read the first line,
you know will never come to
a decent conclusion,
the one that enjambs heedlessly
onward, acting like it's all
stuffed full of suspense and inevitability.
This is the poem that mistakes anaphora
for profundity and tears for seriousness,

that features mysterious stanzas because,
you know, form, or something like it.

This is the poem that appears on Page 42
in every manuscript, every book, every time,
two thirds through and twitching like
a high jumper just before the run-up to the bar,
you liked that metaphor, didn't you?
There won't be another because, see,
that's not what this poem is about.

This poem is about you stopping
being so fucking judgmental
and giving me a fucking break and admitting
I'm a fucking genius without having to prove it
every fucking time.

Ok, I didn't mean that. Ok,
maybe I did.

This poem is just a way
of getting to the next poem.

Please.

JOE NAMATH AT WHOLE FOODS

He was in the pasta aisle.
Holding one of those plastic baskets for when
you just need the one thing and then maybe
some of that cheese with the layer of gray ash
running down the middle or maybe some loose olives
or that fig jam whose price you try not to think about.

And how am I so sure it was him? you might be
wondering, the way I'm also wondering, since I
didn't double back to stare or try to sneak a photo
from my phone. A couple or three things:
First, the socks. Extremely amusing socks. Thin,
extravagantly patterned. Amusing. Then the shoes,
loafers, woven loafers with tassels, who wears
tassels to get the groceries on a weekday
afternoon? And then the glasses, thin gold frames,
very shiny but somehow not ostentatious,
perched on the nose, the unmistakable
Namath nose, big enough for two faces
but owned by one, which has gotten smaller,
making the nose look even larger, but not
unattractive, don't get me wrong. The hair, as usual,
is perfect, white now mostly but still leonine, it says,
"You, on your best day, could never have afforded
to have such perfect hair." And his hair isn't lying.

He is focused, Joe Namath is focused the way
we have seen him focus from several on-field camera angles,
looking down the line of his nose like a gun-sight
at shelves full of pasta boxes. Where is the fusilli?
Was it fusilli I'm looking for? All right then,
where is the goddam rotini?

AMAZONOMACHY

Wherever the Amazons are located by the Greeks, whether it is somewhere
along the Black Sea in the distant north-east, or in Libya in the furthest south, it is
always beyond the confines of the civilized world. The Amazons exist outside the
range of normal human experience.
– Peter Walcot

The story has it that Queen Penthesilea
rides into Troy accompanied by her retinue

of woman warrior Amazons, grief-stricken over
having killed her sister Hippolyta by accident

while they were hunting deer. She wants only to die,
but honorably which means that she has to pick

the losing side. Troy has already lost whatever
was worth losing – Hector is dead and long buried –

but Ajax and Achilles are still around, waiting
for the Iliad to finally end. Ajax

declines to fight but Achilles must be bored or
just decides he needs some exercise and with one

blow to Penthesilea's breastplate knocks her down
and though she pleads for mercy runs her through. This is

where things get complicated. He removes her helmet,
mocks her corpse and then immediately falls in love,

is overcome by lust which he requites there in
the field of battle. This is not what we would call

a helpful precedent in how to get along
with women. There are painters who supposed the Amazons

fought naked to confound their enemies, all those
gleaming white breasts wielding battleaxes and their

bright thighs astride their horses, draped by scarves and manes
appropriately scattered to defend feminine

honor and masculine shame. In all of unrecorded
and recorded myth no Amazon has ever

won the war or even held the field for longer
than a day. Why would a Roman general, thinking

about his unending journey through the uncharted
realms of eternity, order up a truly swell

sarcophagus that corner to corner and end
to end depicts a band of unnamed Amazons

getting the crap kicked out of them by Greeks, also
unnamed, several centuries prior? Apparently

this is a battle that no man can ever lose,
not in the past, not in the future, not in the

sculptor's stone or painter's brush or printer's ink. Surely
the gods will punish us for what we make them do.

MIMESIS

The last two rose canes of November are
    bent over and arched like the backs of borzois,
        the pink buds at their ends like the noses

of borzois sniffing out the spoor of deer
    in a meadow at Yasnaya Polyana
        before the snow begins and makes hunting

problematic, one thing being confused
    with another in what's left of the light.
        We could stop here and let the deer go on

living in the nineteenth century, release
    the roses from simile and metaphor,
        but what would that accomplish? Tolstoy would

only smile and go back to his calisthenics.
    What's the point of literature if you can't
        mistake one thing for another repeatedly

and with purpose? And was any art ever
    not about art, looked at in a certain
        way? I would let you make that argument

pro or con, depending. But I say let
    the roses off the leash in pre-Bolshevik
        Russian November, let them find their way

in the snow and gathering dark, let them
    summon up all their vegetable cunning.
        Let them hunt.

SLIPPAGE

The slippage is sideways, something
holding the ground down has torn loose
and walking forward into a possible
future or backward into a possible past
seems pointless, even if it were
possible to pretend that it was
possible. Everything is rhetoric
and by rhetoric we mean politics
and by politics we mean lies
and by lies we mean rhetoric.

I personally am extremely fond
of rhetoric. It gets me through the day.

Where there used to be pigeons
there are hawks, where there used to be hawks
there are vultures. Scavenge is palpable,
like smoke that never settles. On the edge
of the lagoon, shallow contrivance where
ducks and scullers convene now the ice
is gone for the season, a single coyote strolls
in late morning light, pissing on new grass
and the occasional sapling, staking out
territory, thinking about lunch.

HITLER'S CHILDREN

They'd be about my age, if the war had
turned out a little differently, but
better dressed for sure, even though my parents
practically woke up every morning with
thimbles on their fingers and needles notched

in the lapels of their pajamas, there
being no need for me to be seen petting
the comic dachshund in Berchtesgaden
or standing next to Adolf and Eva
reviewing the victorious troops in

the Alexanderplatz, dressed in itchy
wool shorts and knee socks. Leni Riefenstahl
would have been filming them from birth, with the
idea of a documentary,
something to humanize them all, but stylish.

Their manners would be impeccable, just
like those of the English royal family,
with whom they would have reestablished full
relations, likewise Spain and Portugal
and all the frayed and dissipated threads

of monarchy in France. They still dress well
in France, no matter what the cost. They'd be
grandparents by now, his children, beloved
by all for their willingness to appear
normal and unperturbed by history,

the one thing that the Jews were never good at.
They never would have had what you could call
a real job, other than the customary
royal occupations, sex and philanthropy.
They are not writers, painters or musicians,

at least not publicly. There is no point
in seeking that particular kind of fame
if all your critics can be bought or killed.
They live their lives inside a kind of grace.
They seem to have nothing to be sorry for.

Right from Left

This was the test in second grade:

On the printed workbook page,
spread out flat on my desk like
a map of the world, pick up
your fat school pencil and mark
an X in the box on the right
and a circle in the box on the left,
which I did, quickly, I was quick
with the circles and X's,
which I then erased and reversed
because what if what they really
meant was right and left from
the point of view of the page,
page right and page left, like stage
right and left (which I only
learned about later)? What if what
the world really needed from me
was to turn myself around?

I never got credit for that test
no matter how many ways
I tried to explain. My teacher,
however, in conference with
my mother, did allow as how
even though, at times, I might
appear to be a little slow, there was
no reason yet to give up hope.

PAINTER'S JEANS

This is the secret painting in plain sight,
the one you wear into the studio every day,
the mirror containing all the mistakes
your paintings never make, every smudge,

blot, smear, blob, every wrong choice
or second thought not quite thought through
in deciding how the world this time will end.
Your ankles, your calves, your thighs do not

quite realize how they have been transubstantiated
into the abstract other. The colors, however,
are lovely, denim gesso speckled, layered,
globbed with rose madder, cobalt, Hansa yellow,

phthalocyanine green and a fresh coat of
Payne's gray. The overall effect makes me
think maybe this is what drives painters crazy,
the sight of the impastoed smock at the end of

the day, the fear that what lives on the body
is less a lie than what hangs on the wall.
I think of Pollack in his convertible with his
Long Island cutie, dead drunk in a ditch but

still unquestionably dead, or Rothko flat on
the studio floor, disappearing into the color
field of his own blood, his last painting,
having finally found the ideal shade of red.

A GOOD SCHVITZ

My job as towel boy was to hand out towels
and check their valuables when they came,
as they always came, barring illness or
emergency, to the Nashville JCC

to take a steam at 9 am on Sundays.
This must have been the only time allowed
to them either for forgetting or for
remembering, as long as they could do it

with each other as witness in that slick,
dripping, white tile hot box that no one young
had ever been in or could talk about.
They had all survived the unspeakable war,

the war that still could not be spoken of
as they undressed, some briskly, some slowly,
revealing what survival cost, some ruptured,
some amputated, some scarred from invasive

surgeries, some merely old and naturally
sagging. They took their towels with them into
the schvitz to have something to sit on and
left them there, soggy and fragrant,

for me to pluck up and deposit in
the laundry bin when they were done. This was
a test, I came to gradually realize.
If I could look on them with neither pity

nor horror as they rewound their trusses,
like wrapping phylacteries before prayer,
and covered up their stumps, and emerged in
hats and vests and collars without ties

for Sunday lunch, then there was half a chance
I would myself survive – the evil eye
should now and forever avert its gaze –
and, like them, live to be a tough old Jew.

OLD ELVIS

Without asking us you invented us.
We never knew what we could be
until you showed us on Ed Sullivan

although it was strictly from the waist up.
Ed never believed it for a minute
but he was wrong, wasn't he? Which is why

it hurts now not to have Old Elvis. We got
Young Sun Records Elvis, Army Elvis, Technicolor Elvis,
Skinny White Leather Jumpsuit Elvis, Las Vegas Elvis,

Karate Elvis, Comeback Elvis, Fat White Leather Jumpsuit Elvis,
Sentimental Elvis, Resentful Elvis and finally Dead Elvis.
But no Old Elvis, who would have been useful

in the department of telling us what's next or
how to sing when your pipes have truly
left the building along with a lot of the words.

We never got to see comeback after comeback,
a dozen new cycles of departure and arrival,
each time a little less famous and smelling like

money. It's so clear now – you wanted to
invent music for us but we made you invent sex
instead. And, polite boy that you always were,

you said yes. We did to you what we had done
to Marilyn, who always had to prove she could
actually act. I like to think of you two crossing paths

in some off-season beach town, maybe sitting down
and having that drink you never knew
you always wanted, unrecognizable at last.

Armillaria Gallica

for W. S. Merwin

There is a mushroom growing
underground on the
Upper Peninsula of Michigan,

140 football fields broad,
882,000 lbs.,
2500 years old,

give or take, look it up if you
don't believe me. Although I know
this is not the way it really is,

I like to imagine that all mushrooms
are the one mushroom, that
all gods are the one god,

that all people are the same person,
that all poems are the one
poem and that we have written it

together, are still writing it.
Some things are ridiculous
on the surface and deserve

all the contempt we can manage
to assign them and other things
are best left underground,

felt like the weather but invisible
mostly, nothing much to remind us
that the poem is still being written

and revised in decomposing mold
underfoot, no telling how, when
why, or whether it ends.

A Death on Facebook

for Okla Elliott

Of course I would hear it here
first, or rather experience it

the way we now experience
the weather, the way detail

after detail accretes, providing
eventually a consensus of rain,

in spring, on an afternoon
sidewalk. We knew everything

about you, or so you seemed
to want us to think. We knew

about Bernie and the Pope
and Heidegger and dour,

underappreciated German poets
and your love of Russian soulfulness

and teaching and tacos. We saw
you juggle for your nieces.

You made me want to juggle, too,
if only for myself. What follows

now is not exactly silence but
rather static, a kind of vacant hum.

By quanta or bits or pixels, by any
messenger of the data toward

which we all finally aspire, go
now, Okla, energetically to your rest.

THE RAT'S THANKSGIVING

We have been having this conversation
    for a couple of years now, me trying
to kill you and you finding new ways
    not to die. When I see the pile of
tunnel construction dirt out on the back
    patio, I am enraged and undermined,
too familiar a mood. But this year,
    the day before Thanksgiving, I will not
shove the hose down your hole and try
    to drown you out. Nor will I set out
the green poison pellets where I think
    you might, as if by accident, find them.
I could call my alderwoman to complain
    about rats, your kind, in the alley, but we
have so little faith in government, you
    and I, local or otherwise. On purpose,
we do not discuss each other with
    our families. Rather, it is our job
to pretend that they have never known
    we exist. This is the year I may let you
winter over in peace, with reason to believe
    you may do the same, although at this point
I think it's fair to say we both hope that
    only one of us is still living at Christmas,
one of those holidays that neither of us
    has ever had much real feeling for.

POINSETTIA

Color of cheap wrapping paper and arterial blood,
every year I let you die for my sins. You never
make it past the middle of January, which is when

you start to look needy, requiring cultivation
I'm not prepared to invest in, and you end up
in the bin which is neither paper nor plastic,

the one that should be labeled, "Vaguely Organic,"
like me. I have an aptitude for sacrifice, yours
in particular, although certain others, who are

no longer around, would have stories to tell.
We Jews never should have left the desert,
never should have stopped scaping the goats,

casting them out from our midst, saving the best ones
for sacrifice in the temple, under the altar,
bleeding out under our sacred knives. We should

have stayed savage, dusty, tanned, completely
unreasonable instead of waiting nineteen
hundred years for Europe and Russia to love us.

Instead we grew opportunistic if occasionally
killable. You know, poinsettia, what happens
to those with the best intentions, they become

intoxicated by their own most amusing qualities,
they start to think they're the life of the fucking party
when all along they were only the hired help.

Light Sleeper

The Greek Culture Ministry announced that archaeologists have discovered
the skeletons of a couple positioned as if spooning each other. The prehistoric
remains were unearthed in the cave of Diros in the Peloponnese peninsula in
southern Greece, estimated to have been populated as early as 6,000 BC.
"Double burials in embrace are extremely rare, and that of Diros is one of
the oldest in the world, if not the oldest found to this date," the ministry said.
Scientists carbon-dated the crypt to 3,800 BC, and DNA tests confirmed
that the skeletal remains belong to a young male and female, though their
respective ages were not specified.
– artdaily.org, 4/6/17

I was never what you could call
a light sleeper. Epic though my

snoring might have been, I never
once woke myself up in a shiver of

bewilderment or disgust. I slept through
it all, the rages, the frantic pacing,

the weary despair, the plain hatred,
like the male cat does when the female

crawls off into the closet to give birth.
But I did so like your head nestled

in that concavity between chest and
shoulder when you finally came

to rest, your hair a private ocean I
could float in. The trouble is

I habitually twitch as I fall backward
into sleep, as though reaching out

for a handhold on the night, which
only wakes you into new annoyance

and poisons the coming day. It's
much better like this, arranged as

complementary parts of the same
machine, facing the same way as if

agreeing for once about what is past
and what is future. And so you are held

yourself without having to hold, an
answer to a question you never knew

you could ask. There were problems
from the start, but when are there

ever not? We couldn't change each
other so we became each other, our

faults absorbed into every opposite pore,
each opposing bone. When we are

discovered, when our version of
eternity comes to an end, our

hope was that what we had thought
was our virtue but was only our love,

only our attachment, will be set free,
will be let out into the light.

III

Olivetti Lettera 22, Red

I never had you when I could have,
sitting there on a thick plexiglass shelf

with tasteful, concealed lighting in the
Olivetti showroom on Fifth Avenue,

a holy kind of space where each
writer of type could be walked around

and gawked at like a Lamborghini
or a Maserati. I was only being faithful,

I told myself, to my medium blue IBM
Correcting Selectric, squatting on

my desk like an overweight mistress,
waiting for me to get home and

finally write something for chrissake.
You were too beautiful to be practical

and, worse, I couldn't quite afford you.
It wouldn't have been fair to either

one of us in the end. But I like to
think, still, about what might have

happened with my fingers on your keys.
You were so beautiful. You still are.

CATCHING MY BREATH

I used to run
out in front
confident that she
would catch up to me
eventually
no place I could
think to go
she wouldn't follow
like an obedient
shadow permanently
attached to what
moves under the sun

now I follow along
behind sometimes almost
within grasp of her
sometimes barely able
to recognize my breath
taking a nap under a tree
on the horizon line
or conspiring with
my same shadow my
familiars my reputation
about what life might hold
for them without me

my breath has made it
clear to me she
will never again
let herself be caught
close as I might come

to sneaking up on her for
an awkward embrace
unlike myself my breath
has made definite
plans for the future
is more than ready for
whatever comes next

JIMI VS. WOLFGANG

for Derek Bermel

I think of the first time Wolfgang Amadeus heard Jimi
playing *The Wind Cries Mary* and saying out loud,

"Was für Scheisse sind diese Wörte? Die Musik, aber…"
(rough translation: "These lyrics are pure crap. The music,

however…"). It's true, you know, the lyrics never did
make any sense, something about a fight with his

girlfriend. But honestly, who really cares what
The Queen of the Night is saying when she hits her

high note? All those operas were just another way
to get paid, not that there was ever anything wrong

with that. The music will have its way with you and
ostinato is still ostinato and what goes around comes

around and could any of us take another living breath
without rubato, could we listen to John Philip Sousa

covering James Brown on his Christmas album without
wanting to blow our brains out? I don't think so.

TOURISTS

In the museum of departures
we left it all behind.

In the museum of arrivals
we felt the anxiety of the utterly dispossessed.
We were not the utterly dispossessed.

In the museum of constant crying
we wept.

In the museum of food
we had the flan.

In the museum of trees
we stole a leaf. No,
we stole a whole branch.

In the museum of giving birth
we gave.

In the museum of philosophy –
we did not go to the museum of philosophy.

In the museum of architecture
high on a promontory above the diminutive city
and the river dividing it like a shiny vector
we longed for a cigarette.

In the museum of remembrance
we discovered our names on the wall of engraved names.
In pencil.

In the museum of God
we grew tired of looking up.

In the museum of good intentions
we stayed until closing time.

In the museum of sex
I made you laugh.

TRAIN WRECK, MINNEAPOLIS (A LOVE POEM)

I felt the sound before I heard it,
a cone of noise with vast ambition
but nothing in back of it but silence,
the kind that comes after calamity.

The train stopped short after
having dragged the car catty-corner
into the crossing. The point of impact
was the front passenger door and

window, shards of which were
being pulled delicately out of the
arm and shoulder of the woman
who sat on the curb, blood, but

not too much blood, leaking into
a handkerchief wrapped around
her wrist. The boy still sat quietly
in the backseat, thinking about

the continuous collisions he rehearsed
with toy train and toy train,
toy car and toy truck, toy car and
toy train until the man came and

plucked him up into the world again,
where, in the distance, you could hear
sirens, many sirens approach
and converge. Does it matter that

this was the same train on the same track
that I was planning to take later
to the airport? No, it does not.
And what was the man thinking
who drove his family across the tracks?

What thought could possibly be big enough
for him to lose track of a train? Driving along,
I've had that same thought myself.

Lucky, I guess, to know a woman
who won't think twice about
yelling at me, you fool, before I go and
drive us off the edge of the earth.

23 AND NOT ME

I want to know everything but
more specifically I could give a fuck about
which square foot of what miserable shtetl my great, great,
great grandparents were driven out of and what
miserable shtetl they ended up in.

Or whether I am
1/64th part cannibal or Glaswegian.
I still can't dance.

What I'd like to find out is whether
in a past life I fled the ramparts of a burning castle
or spent a few cycles as an ever-larger
species of lizard. That would account
for inexplicable feelings about fire and heights
and, as reported by others, a certain cold-bloodedness.

Even farther back is fine – protozoa, ectoplasm,
unarrived light from an infinitely distant star,
the very breath of God.

I'll swab that swab or spit in that cup,
I'll FedEx you a good handful of excrement
if we can only get down to cases, find out
what is really wrong.

CLAY HORSES

I have two, Han Dynasty by attribution but in truth
that may only be their blood line. I didn't care,
that's how it is when you fall in love with a horse,
something in you has to have it. And they are attainable,

if indifferent, whatever the price. I started out early,
drawing pencil stick figures not of family but TV
horseflesh, constant companions on Saturday morning,
hardly ever stars as such and totally innocent of plot.

Then came crayon drawings, entire boxes of Crayolas
worn to nubs on laundry shirt cardboard. The horses began
to take on weight and feature after feature – hooves, teeth,
mains, tails, nostrils, ears, eyes, fetlocks – posture.

Then in first grade came clay, which I discovered was
free and in addition to black, white, blue, green and gray,
was available in a particular bisque shade the precise color
of palomino pony skin. I had found my medium at last

and commenced a practice. You could have opened a gallery –
The First Grade Clay Horse Gallery – with what I made
until they took the clay away. It was astonishing but odd.
Feature by feature horses began to fade from my dream,

replaced by bicycles and skates, attainable in theory and
no more likely to be discovered grazing by the front porch
than a palomino pony. But disappointment should never
be confused with failure. Bicycles and skates came

and went and horses would wait, not patiently,
as patience is not in their nature, but with equanimity
and a kind of grace. I look forward to seeing them now,
perched high up on the china cabinet, when I come home.

If they are in truth Han Dynasty, as the horse trader
I bought them from said, then they have come far enough.
If I could find the key to my dream, I would let them in
by the north gate, there to pasture as long as they like.

WAILING WALL

This is what's left
of the second temple
forget the first although

iceberg-like it goes on
forever underground with
tunnels and chambers

and aqueducts ancient
gears and levers
a vast factory for

holiness which is all
it was ever meant
to produce now the wall

a single serried
row of stones accepts its
supplicants its fanatics

its tourists its devout
and its indifferent
equally take a piece

of paper write down
whatever prayer it is
you're most willing

to not have answered
stick it in
the space between

one stone and the next
and wait a lifetime
or go underground

walk along a path
excavated for your benefit
narrow though it may be

follow your guide
and emerge centuries
later through a hole

in the middle of
East Jerusalem where
as you walk back

through the market
and to the west you
discover in the eyes

of every vendor that
you also are the answer
to no one's prayer

THE OLD POETS IN LINE AT THE URINALS
AT THE WRITERS' CONFERENCE

Since there are only fifteen minutes between
the end of one panel and the beginning
of the next, they come running, although truth

to tell, few can actually still run,
to get their chance to stand before the bright
white porcelain concavities we seem

to be so much the better at producing
than the French have ever been. We are not
thinking of Marcel Duchamp as we stand there,

dangling our penises absent-mindedly,
like scarred old tools that, once we have them in
our hands again, we half-expect to know

the secrets of life. We are also not thinking
about the young poets in line behind us
trying not to look impatient or annoyed.

Their time is coming, although not before
we shake off the last drop, zip up and flush,
assuming we remember to do all three,

assuming we can finish what we started
so long ago with such imperfect knowledge
and animal enthusiasm. For now,

however, we stand as one, an ancient navy
at the bright tile wall, trying to visualize
the ocean, trying to call forth the tide.

SHARDS

It had to happen
more shards than pots
no more counting up
from one
just counting down
to zero
past zero
finally feeling what
negative numbers
feel like on
my negative fingers
there are seedlings
you keep insisting
there may yet
be flowers I admit
but you could have
told me how it is
I say
I did tell you
how it was
you said
you could have lied
then
I say
I did lie
you said

ODE TO CLAES OLDENBURG

Tear down the statues
the hollow metal men
who won the war
who lost the war
but fought so unreasonably

bravely and the horses
they rode in on
haul off the humble infantrymen
at parade rest now the
battle has passed them by

and the great leaders
pointing toward the future
which is now a parking lot
but leave the pedestals
let us come into full

understanding of absence
of negative intention
of not having a clue
about what happens
next let us instead

erect an eggbeater
a pencil an eraser
a garden spade and
a garden hose a baseball
bat a saw a book of

matches a shuttlecock
a pair of pliers an apple
core in their places
let us forget we have
history and how we got it

history which always runs
back to our open hands
faithful dog clenching
the past in its teeth
like a wet smelly stick

Gazebo

for Tony Hoagland

It's raining but the birds
still have to go to work.

No one has given them the day off
or dropped a handful of seed

in the attractive but abandoned
birdhouse. After long illness,

a poet has died and a flock
of turkey buzzards

wheels overhead as though
they were a squadron of

fighter jets at the Superbowl
before getting down to

the business of finding something
that smells sufficiently dead.

The gazebo is empty, but then
the gazebo is always empty,

emptiness and foolish, beautiful,
romantic, unpractical thinking

being the only reasons
it could ever have existed

in the first place, and on its roof,
the weathervane, which has

soldered-on letters that say,
N, S, E, and W, is spinning slowly

and pointing in every direction,
just the way you used to like to do.

PIECEWORK

... just because you don't know what work is.
– Philip Levine

It's a way of dealing with
lack of ambition,

a way to close off
the view of the big picture

which always threatens
in that moment between

the dream's closing credits
and the open eye's

claim on your day.
My parents took in piecework

their whole lives
because it was a living.

I do it, too. No novels
for me, with time like

a bolt of navy blue worsted
stretched from one end

to the other. Rather a few
shapely but elastic lines

draped on stanzas as though
on hangers, made to be

taken out and worn on
weekends, and in the right

artificial light, acknowledged
as inevitable, if not perfect.

IT IS NOT YET SPRING

It is not yet spring but
Leonard Cohen is singing
in the car in French. I can't
understand a single word
but I'm guessing the song
is either about regret or total
lack of regret. Even I can tell
his accent isn't terrific.
There are young people
out on the streets and
some of them are dressed
in a manner I would consider
inappropriate if they were
my children but they are
not my children, they are
their own uniquely amazing
creations, never seen anything
like them, not here in Chicago.
Leonard Cohen sounds
miserable and therefore
completely satisfied with
himself, he is, after all,
singing in his bad accent
and that makes me
completely happy and
the young people, who
cannot hear him because
the windows are rolled up
and, even though they
might tell you otherwise,
cannot yet have felt
much about regret or
the total lack of regret and
are dressed a little casually,
in my opinion, considering
the actual weather, are all
convinced, I'm sure of it,
they will live forever.

THE COMPANY OF DUCKS

They are not indifferent
just busy they have
other affairs
to attend to
paddling for example
upstream in a bunch
or a raft
which is also called
redundantly a paddling
they plunge their whole heads
under rhythmically
seeking whatever it is
that ducks eat
reminding you of
the first time you
willingly stuck your head
underwater Nashville
Sevier Park public pool
lessons for how to be
in the water perhaps
one day to float
perhaps another to
paddle like a dog
perhaps to adapt
successfully like other
mammals otters polar bears
whales to a new element
perhaps to evolve I was
never made to feel
at home in the water
though I could tread
with the best of treaders
never was I at ease
yet here on the bank
of a shallow river
I am glad for the company
of ducks glad to know
if I didn't already know it
that to be ignored
is not to be alone

LEAF

Not the green thing,
the engine of
photosynthesis, or
a page from a book
you once wrote,
are still writing,
but the thing that,
when you remember
exactly how
to separate the table,
lets your life fit

when your life
sits down to eat,
the thing that sometime
between the end
of dinner and

the beginning
of going to bed,
must be carried
back upstairs,
reminding you
that yes,
your life is heavy,
as it was surely
meant to be,
and on occasion
requires assistance

CATERPILLAR

I send you this photograph of a caterpillar
from Virginia. He, or she – how would I ever know? –

is impossibly fuzzy, perhaps a sign of harsher
than normal winter lurking in the hills
where they ride horses and hunt deer.

The caterpillar has not yet found out that they
are shooting Jews in Pittsburgh, right in the middle

of Saturday morning services. They will not
have had the chance to put the Torah away
yet, to wrap it up like a perpetually well-behaved

baby and sing it back to sleep in its velvet-lined ark,
or to hear a sermon on how to heal the world,

much less to say a prayer for the anniversaries
of the deaths of all their dead relatives. They
won't be getting around to that this morning

in the Tree of Life Synagogue in Pittsburgh,
where Jews go to remind themselves that whatever

happened once can and will happen again
and where, if it were an actual tree, caterpillars
will emerge in the spring, dangling from newly

green leaves, preparing themselves as best
they can remember how to become something
that sheds history like a sad old coat and takes flight.

ACKNOWLEDGMENTS

The author thanks Susan Gardner and Mark Hudson for bringing this volume to light; the Atlantic Center for the Arts, Vermont Studio Center, and the Virginia Center for the Creative Arts, where much of this work was begun; forbearing readers and occasional listeners Heather McHugh, Joan Houlihan, Natania Rosenfeld, Paula Lambert, Elizabeth Jacobson, and Anna V.Q. Ross; the usual gang at Posey and Marv's; and Karen, who accords me the great honor of liking me best.

UNPRACTICAL THINKING is set in Gill Sans, designed by Eric Gill.
It was adopted by British Railways.